MITZIE WILSON AND NICHOLA PALMER

CHOCOLATE COOKERY

HAMLYN

First published in 1986 by
Hamlyn Publishing
Bridge House, London Road,
Twickenham, Middlesex, England

Produced by New Leaf Productions

Photography by Mick Duff
Design by Jim Wire
Typeset by System Graphics Ltd., Folkestone
Edited by Josephine Bacon

ISBN 0 600 32636 5

Printed in Spain

Lito. A. Romero, S. A. - D. L. TF. 391 – 1986

NOTE
All spoons are level, unless otherwise specified.
Metric and imperial measurements have been
calculated separately; use one set of
measurements only, as they are not exact
equivalents.

We would like to thank:
Anne Haycock for typing the manuscript; Stephanie
Culham and Tricia Payne for helping with
photography; Mrs Joan Wilkes and Mrs Meg
Palmer for the loan of props and Donald Brown and
Glyn Palmer for being keen recipe tasters.

CONTENTS

Introduction 4
Melting chocolate 6
Piping chocolate 7
Chocolate decorations 8
Chocolate cakes 10
Hot puddings and desserts 18
Cold desserts and ice creams 24
Biscuits 38
Confectionery 46
Sauces and icings 52
Drinks 56
Chocolate novelties 58
Index 64

INTRODUCTION

Both cocoa and chocolate are made from roasted ground cocoa beans. Chocolate is made by adding extra cocoa butter and sugar to the beans. The higher the percentage of cocoa solids, the darker and stronger the flavour of the chocolate. You will find the recipes in this book use the most widely available plain and milk chocolates but there is a wide choice available.

Plain Dark Chocolate with a high proportion of cocoa solids, has a rich, bittersweet flavour. It melts easily and sets hard, so it is ideal for piping and moulding.

Milk Chocolate, is paler, as it contains less cocoa and added milk. Being a softer chocolate, it does not set so hard.

White Chocolate is not really chocolate at all, though it is made from cocoa butter. It contains no cocoa solids but has full-cream milk and sugar added. It is difficult to melt and is better dissolved in another liquid, such as milk.

Unsweetened Chocolate, also called *Dessert Chocolate* although it contains some sugar has a high proportion of cocoa solids, giving a bittersweet flavour. It is rather expensive, but is worth using for decoration as it melts easily and sets very hard, smooth and shiny. It can be used in most recipes provided you adjust the amount of sugar to taste. The best varieties come from France.

Chocolate-flavoured Cake Covering or *Cooking Chocolate.* Available in bars or dots. It can't legally be called chocolate — it's really a mixture of vegetable oil, cocoa powder and sugar. Both plain and milk chocolate cake covering can be used in our recipes, but bear in mind the flavour will not be as rich as that of real chocolate.

Couverture: A rich-flavoured chocolate with a high proportion of cocoa butter, which makes it hard and shiny. It has to be tempered for the best results, which means heating it and cooling it, heating it and cooling it again, until all the cocoa solids and butter melt out. It is expensive and mostly used by professional caterers.

Dipping Chocolate is also a professional catering product, which is difficult to find. It has a high proportion of vegetable fats and melts to a thinner consistency, ideal for coating or dipping confectionery.

Cocoa is the powder left after much of the cocoa butter has been extracted from the roasted beans. Dissolve cocoa powder in hot water for use in recipes, or for cake making, substitute tablespoons of flour with cocoa and simply sift it into mixture.

Drinking Chocolate is cocoa with added sugar and emulsifiers to make it dissolve more easily. It is *not* suitable as a replacement for cocoa in recipes.

Carob is a chocolate substitute which is free from caffeine and contains less oxalic acid (which sometimes causes skin blemishes). It tastes similar to chocolate but is not so creamy or rich. Carob powder always needs sifting but can be used instead of cocoa in cakes and desserts. Just substitute one for the other. Carob bars do not melt so easily as chocolate. It is best to melt carob in liquid.

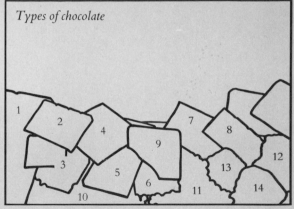

Types of chocolate

KEY 1, Couverture 2, Plain Dark Chocolate 3, Milk Chocolate 4, White Chocolate 5, Plain Cooking Chocolate 6, Milk Cooking Chocolate 7, Dairy-free Chocolate 8, Carob Bar 9, Dessert Chocolate 10, Cooking Chocolate Dots 11, Dipping Chocolate 12, Carob Powder 13, Cocoa Powder 14, Drinking Chocolate

MELTING CHOCOLATE

The safest way to melt chocolate is to grate it finely and place in a dry heat-proof bowl. Stand the bowl over a saucepan of hot, but not boiling, water and leave to melt, stirring occassionally. If the chocolate stiffens and loses its gloss it means the chocolate overheated, the water was too hot, the bowl was touching the water, or steam got into the chocolate. To try and rectify the situation add 1 teaspoon cooking oil for every 25 g/1 oz chocolate and beat well. White chocolate, in particular, must always be grated as it needs little heat to melt. If white chocolate overheats, add a little boiling water and beat well.

Chocolate can be successfully melted in a micro-wave oven; timings will vary with the quantity of chocolate and wattage of the oven. Break chocolate into pieces and place in a suitable bowl. Melt on a medium-to-low setting for a few seconds at a time, and check frequently.

Where a recipe requires liquid to be mixed with melted chocolate the liquid should be placed in the bowl and the chocolate melted in it. When stirred, they will blend together. Do not try to add liquid after the chocolate has melted, or the mixture will stiffen.

Cocoa

If cocoa is to be used in an uncooked recipe, e.g. butter icing or glacé icing, it should be slightly 'cooked' beforehand to give a better flavour. This is easily done by mixing the cocoa with sufficient boiling water to make a thick paste. The cocoa can then be easily blended into the other ingredients in the recipe.

PIPING CHOCOLATE

Greaseproof paper icing bags are the best to use, primarily because you don't have to wash them up. To make a greaseproof icing bag fold a 25-cm/10-inch square of greaseproof paper in half diagonally. Roll point A over point C. Roll point B to behind C. Fold down the points to secure the bag.

When making a greaseproof paper icing bag for piping chocolate, do not snip off the end to make the nozzle until you have poured chocolate into the bag. Spoon melted chocolate into the piping bag, fold down the top, and then snip off the tip to allow the chocolate to come through (no metal or plastic piping nozzle is required). To drizzle chocolate, pipe zig-zag lines over the item to be decorated. To make butterflies, swans, flowers and other lacework designs, trace outlines on plain paper and cover with waxed paper. Fill piping bag as above and snip off the point. Pipe shapes following the outlines. Leave to set, and carefully peel off waxed paper. Always make more designs than required to allow for breakages.

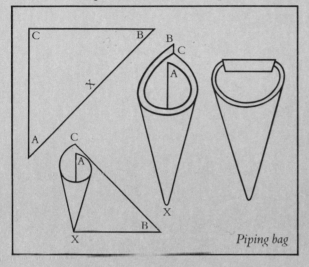

Piping bag

CHOCOLATE DECORATIONS

Chocolate Shapes

Spread melted chocolate onto greaseproof paper or non-stick baking parchment and allow to set at room temperature. The chocolate should not be chilled or it will shatter when cut. Using pastry cutters, or a sharp knife and a ruler, cut out squares, triangles, rounds, hearts, stars etc. Store in a covered container until required.

Chocolate Scrolls (Caraque)

Grate 75 g/3 oz plain chocolate and melt in a bowl over a pan of hot water with 25 g/1 oz butter and 2 teaspoons water. Stir until smooth. Alternatively melt milk or plain chocolate. Spread the chocolate thinly on a laminated or marble surface. Leave until just set. Using a long, sharp knife shave the chocolate slant-wise; use a slight sawing movement and hold the knife at an angle. The chocolate should curl into long scrolls. Keep in a cool place until required.

Chocolate Shavings

Hold a bar of chocolate at room temperature in one hand and with the other hand peel off shavings of chocolate with a potato peeler.

Grated Chocolate

Grate coarsely or finely as required.

Chocolate Leaves

Brush a coating of melted chocolate over the underside of rose leaves or bay leaves. Leave to set, then carefully peel off the leaf.

Chocolate Shells

Polish plastic shell moulds (available from most cook shops) with cotton wool. Brush melted plain dark chocolate into the mould and leave to cool. Repeat this process until the chocolate reaches the required thickness (3-mm/⅛-inch). Allow to set firmly in a cool place. Turn out of mould and use to decorate ice creams, gateaux, etc.

Chocolate Cups

Use a double thickness of paper petits fours cases or paper cake cases. brush melted chocolate over the inside of the paper cases. Leave to set. For the larger cases, brush on a second layer of chocolate. Keep cool until required.

CHOCOLATE CONES
Makes 4

100 g/4 oz chocolate

Fold and cut a 25-cm/10-inch square in half diagonally then in half diagonally again to make 4 small equal triangles. Make into piping bags (see page 7) and staple the bag to keep its shape. Trim the open end of piping bag to make the top of the cone circular. Melt the chocolate and brush it inside the cones, using a small, clean paintbrush. Turn cones upside down on a wire rack until set and carefully peel away paper.

CHOCOLATE ROSES
Makes about 12 roses

Very effective for decorating gâteaux and birthday cakes and really quite simple to make. Buy liquid glucose from chemist's.

100 g/4 oz cooking chocolate, grated
75 g/3 oz liquid glucose

Melt the chocolate in a bowl over a pan of hot water. Heat the liquid glucose in a separate bowl over another pan of hot water. Gradually beat the warm liquid glucose into the chocolate until smooth. Leave to cool. Cover and store in the fridge. To make a rose: make a coned shape to use as the base. Then take a small piece of the chocolate mixture the size of a pea flatten and pinch it into a circular petal between finger and thumb or if your hands become too warm, place inside a heavy duty polythene bag or between 2 pieces of polythene. (The wrapping from processed cheese is ideal. Cut it into 2 squares — wash and dry it well). Roll thinly with a rolling pin and wrap around the cone. Repeat, overlapping the petals, until you have a rose. Make leaves by rolling and cutting out oval shapes. Mark them with veins and allow to dry in a curved shape. Store any remaining chocolate mixture in the fridge.

CHOCOLATE CAKES

ALL-IN-ONE CHOCOLATE CAKE

12 servings

A simple and quick everyday cake to fill and top with jam, cream, icing. Alternatively serve with custard or chocolate sauce, as a pudding.

175 g/6 oz self-raising flour
2 tablespoons cocoa
1½ teaspoons baking powder
175 g/6 oz soft margarine
175 g/6 oz caster sugar
3 eggs, size 2

Set oven at 180°C, 350°F, gas 4. Brush baking tins or bowl (see below) with melted fat or oil and line bases with greased greaseproof paper. Sift flour, cocoa and baking powder in a bowl and add margarine, sugar and eggs. Mix together with a wooden spoon, then beat for 2–3 minutes until mixture is smooth and glossy (this will only take 1–2 minutes in an electric mixer or between 30 seconds and 1 minute in a food processor). Place the mixture in prepared tins or bowl and level the top with the back of a spoon. Bake in the centre of the oven (the cooking times depend on the size and type of baking tin used, and are given below). To test the cake when cooked gently press it with your fingers. If cooked, the cake should spring back and have just begun to shrink from the sides of the tin. Allow to cool for 5 minutes before loosening the sides of the cake from the tin. Turn out onto a wire rack.

To remove a cake easily from a ring tin, lay a damp cloth over the top of the hot tin and cake will release. This mixture is sufficient for:—

Cake Tin Size	Approx. Cooking Time
2 20-cm/8-inch sandwich tins	35–40 minutes
2 23-cm/9-inch sandwich tins	25 minutes
2 15-cm/6-inch deep cake tins	45–50 minutes
1 18-cm/7-inch deep square tin	45–50 minutes
1 28 × 18-cm/11 × 7-inch Swiss roll tin	35–40 minutes
1 1.2-litre/2-pint basin (omit baking powder)	1¼–1½ hours
23-cm/9-inch ring tin	45–50 minutes
12 individual paper cake cases	15–20 minutes

LEMON RIPPLE CAKE
6 Servings

This cake is baked with its filling and topping all together — a definite time saver.

225 g/8 oz plain flour
pinch of salt
2 teaspoons baking powder
75 g/3 oz margarine
75 g/3 oz caster sugar
1 egg
2 teaspoons grated lemon rind
150 ml/¼ pint milk
100 g/4 oz plain chocolate, coarsely grated
  sifted icing sugar to decorate

Grease a 15-cm/6-inch round cake tin and line the base with greased greaseproof paper. Sift the flour, salt and baking powder into a mixing bowl. Rub the margarine into the flour until mixture resembles fine breadcrumbs. Add the sugar, egg, lemon rind and milk, and stir with a wooden spoon until smooth; the mixture should have a soft dropping consistency. Spoon a third of the cake mixture into the prepared tin and sprinkle a third of the chocolate over the top. Add another layer of cake mixture and sprinkle with chocolate, and so on, finishing with a layer of chocolate. Bake in a preheated oven at 190°C, 375°F, gas 5 for 15 minutes, then reduce heat to 180°C, 350°F, gas 4 for a further hour. Cool on a wire rack. Sprinkle with icing sugar.

CHOCOLATE CUP CAKES
18 cup cakes

Just like the ones you enjoyed as kids! Spread the icing over the cakes (still in their cases) while they are still quite hot.

100 g/4 oz block margarine, softened
100 g/4 oz caster sugar
2 eggs
75 g/3 oz self-raising flour
25 g/1 oz cocoa
½ quantity chocolate fudge icing (see page 53)

Line bun tins with 18 paper cake cases. Place all the cake ingredients in a bowl and beat together with a wooden spoon for 2 to 3 minutes until smooth and glossy (1 to 2 minutes in an electric mixer). Place 1 rounded teaspoon of mixture in base of each cake case and bake in centre of a (180°C, 350°F, gas 4) oven for 10 to 15 minutes, or until firm to touch. Leave to cool.

Make the icing as directed on p 53. Pour it over the cup cakes and allow to set. If the mixture begins to set or becomes grainy, place it over a low heat and allow to melt again. Store in a cake tin for up to 2 weeks.

DEVIL'S FOOD CAKE
10 servings

A not-too-sweet, firm cake, ideal as a base of many novelty cakes. This American cake is iced with Chocolate Fudge Icing. (See recipe page 53).

75 g/3 oz cocoa powder
350 ml/12 fl oz boiling water
175 g/6 oz butter
275 g/10 oz granulated sugar
3 eggs, beaten
275 g/10 oz plain flour
1½ teaspoons bicarbonate of soda
¼ teaspoon baking powder

Grease a deep, round 23-cm/9-inch cake tin and line it with greased greaseproof paper. Dissolve the cocoa in the boiling water. Allow to cool.

Cream the butter and sugar until pale and creamy. Then gradually beat in the eggs. Sift the flour, bicarbonate of soda and baking powder. Fold the flour and cocoa mixture alternately into the creamed mixture. Pour this into the cake tin and bake in moderate oven (180°C, 350°F, gas 4) for 1½ hours or, until firm to the touch. Turn out, and place upside down on a wire rack to cool. Then cut the cake in half. Sandwich and top the cake with chocolate Fudge Icing (see page 53)

CAROB YOGURT CAKE
8–10 servings

A rich moist cake made with carob for those who prefer it to chocolate for dietary reasons.

150 ml/¼ pint vegetable oil
150 ml/¼ pint natural yogurt
4 tablespoons golden syrup
100 g/4 oz muscovado sugar
3 eggs
225 g/8 oz self-raising wholemeal flour
3 rounded tablespoons carob powder
½ teaspoon salt
2 tablespoons sunflower seeds

Grease and line a square 20–cm/8-inch cake tin. Place the oil, yogurt, syrup, sugar and eggs in a bowl; beat with a wooden spoon until well mixed. Stir the flour, carob powder, and salt into bowl; mix well. Pour the mixture into the prepared tin, sprinkle with sunflower seeds and bake in the centre of a preheated oven at 160°C, 325°F, gas 3 for 1 hour 15 minutes to 1 hour 30 minutes until firm to the touch. Leave cake to cool in the tin, then turn it out and remove the paper. To store the cake, wrap it in foil and keep it for two or three days to bring out the full flavour. Then store it for up to 1 week in a tin.

BANANA AND CHOCOLATE CAKE

Make sure you use mottled brown, ripe bananas for this rich, moist recipe.

175 g/6 oz margarine
225 g/8 oz granulated sugar
2 large ripe bananas
1 teaspoon vanilla essence
275 g/10 oz self-raising flour
½ teaspoon salt
½ teaspoon bicarbonate of soda
2 eggs
50 g/2 oz chocolate chips
50 g/2 oz sweetened banana chips

Grease a 1.15 litre (2 pint) loaf tin. Line the base and sides with greased greaseproof paper. Place the margarine and sugar in a saucepan and cook over a low heat until margarine has just melted. Remove pan from heat. Peel the bananas, weigh out 225 g/8 oz of them and place them in a shallow bowl with the vanilla essence; mash until smooth. Sift the flour, salt and bicarbonate of soda into a bowl. Add to the mixture in the pan, and mix with a wooden spoon. Beat the eggs and add to the pan with the banana; mix well. Fold in the chocolate chips; do not over mix.

Place the mixture in prepared tin and level top with the back of a metal spoon. Sprinkle with banana chips and bake the cake in the centre of a moderate (160°C, 325°F, gas 3) oven for 1 hour 40 minutes to 1 hour 50 minutes until firm to the touch.

Leave the cake to cool in the tin, then turn it out and remove the greaseproof paper. Wrap the cake in foil and store it for two or three days to allow flavour to develop. The cake will keep well up to two weeks if wrapped in foil and placed in a tin.

CHOCOLATE FRUIT AND NUT CAKE
12 servings

Choc-a-bloc full of whole nuts, plump apricots and cherries. Do use maraschino cherries if you can, they're a lovely moist surprise-in-the-mouth!

100 g/4 oz butter
100 g/4 oz caster sugar
50 g/2 oz cocoa powder
175 g/6 oz plain flour
4 eggs, beaten
100-g/4-oz jar maraschino cherries
225 g/8 oz multi-coloured glacé cherries
275 g/10 oz mixed, whole, shelled nuts – brazil nuts, walnuts, hazelnuts, cashews, etc.
175 g/6 oz dried apricots, quartered

Icing and Decoration:
2 egg whites
2 rounded tablespoons liquid glucose
About 500 g/1 lb icing sugar, sifted
100 g/4 oz cocoa powder
3 tablespoons apricot jam
23-cm/9-inch cake board

Grease and line a deep 19-cm/7-inch cake tin. Cream the butter and sugar until light and fluffy. Sift the cocoa and flour together, and fold into creamed mixture alternately with the eggs. Drain the maraschino cherries, reserving the syrup. Stir the maraschino cherries, glacé cherries, nuts and apricots into creamed mixture with 2 tablespoons of the syrup. Mix well and place in the cake tin. Smooth top of cake. Bake at 180°C, 350°F, gas 4 for 1½ hours to 1 hour 40 minutes until firm to the touch. Leave to cool in the tin.

Place the cake on a 23-cm/9-inch cake board. Spread the top and sides of the cake with the jam.

Mix the egg whites with the cocoa, glucose and enough icing sugar to make soft paste. Dust a work surface with icing sugar. Roll out the paste icing on the work surface, making it large enough to cover the cake. Drape the icing over a rolling pin and transfer it to the cake. Smooth it down over the sides and trim off any excess. Knead the trimmings into a ball. Roll and cut out four 35 × 28-cm/14 × 16-inch strips of icing. Place two across the cake like a parcel. Cut the remaining two strips in half. Loop two strips around a piece of kitchen paper for support and place at the centre of the cake. Cut 'v' shapes at one end of each of the remaining two strips and place them on the cake to complete the bow. Allow to dry then remove the paper.

BLACK FOREST BARS
16 slices

Rather like bakewell tart—moist and almondy. Use apricot jam and well-drained, canned apricots as an alternative to the black cherry jam and glacé cherries. The mixture, minus the icing, can be served as a pudding, with custard.

Pastry:
150 g/5 oz plain flour
75 g/3 oz block margarine or butter, cut into pieces
25 g/1 oz caster sugar
1 size 4 egg, lightly beaten
4 tablespoons black cherry or red jam

Cake:
75 g/3 oz self-raising flour
1 teaspoon baking powder
2 tablespoons cocoa powder
100 g/4 oz ground almonds
100 g/4 oz caster sugar
100 g/4 oz margarine
1 teaspoon almond flavouring
2 eggs, lightly beaten

Icing:
275 g/10 oz icing sugar, sifted
1 teaspoon cocoa
1 teaspoon boiling water
8 glacé cherries

Grease a 28 × 18 × 2.5-cm/11 × 7 × 1-inch baking tin. Place the flour in a bowl; add the margarine or butter, and rub in with the fingertips until mixture resembles fine breadcrumbs. Add the sugar and stir. Make a well in centre, add the beaten egg and mix with a fork to form a soft dough. Knead the dough lightly, wrap it in cling film and chill for 30 minutes until firm.

Roll out pastry into rectangle 5-cm/2-inches larger than baking tin. Support the pastry on a rolling pin and lift it into the tin. Gently ease the pastry onto the base and up the sides of the tin. Trim off the surplus with a sharp knife. Spread the jam on the pastry base.

To make the cake, place the flour, baking powder, cocoa, ground almonds, sugar, margarine, flavouring and eggs in a bowl. Mix together with a wooden spoon, then beat for 2 to 3 minutes (1 to 2 minutes, if using an electric mixer), until the mixture is smooth and glossy. Spread it in the tin and level the top with back of a metal spoon. Bake in the centre of a moderately hot oven at 190°C, 375°F, gas 5 for 35 to 40 minutes until risen and firm to the touch. Leave the mixture to cool in a tin for 10 minutes, then turn it out and cool it completely on a wire rack.

Sift the icing sugar into a bowl. Gradually add a little hot water until the icing thickly coats the back of a spoon. Place 4 tablespoons of the icing in a separate bowl and reserve it. Coat cake with remaining icing. Mix the cocoa with boiling water and stir into the reserved icing. Place this mixture in a small, greaseproof paper piping bag. Use a sharp knife to mark the top of cake into 16 bars. Cut the glacé cherries in half and place one at the end of each bar. Snip the end off the piping bag and pipe a stalk and leaf for each cherry. Allow the icing to set for 1 hour before cutting into bars.

BLACK FOREST GATEAU
14 servings

Sponge:
6 eggs, separated
150 g/5 oz caster sugar
50 g/2 oz plain flour, sifted
75 g/3 oz cornflower, sifted
50 g/2 oz cocoa, sifted

Biscuit Base:
150 g/5 oz plain flour
1 egg yolk
75 g/3 oz caster sugar
150 g/5 oz butter

Filling and Topping:
425-g/15-oz can pitted black cherries
2 teaspoons arrowroot
8 tablespoons Kirsch
3 tablespoons redcurrant jelly
450 ml/¾ pint double cream

To decorate:
Chocolate caraque and grated chocolate

Grease a 23-cm/9-inch loose-bottomed cake tin and line it with greased greaseproof paper. Whisk the egg yolks with 6 tablespoons of hand-hot water and the caster sugar until thick and mousse-like. The mixture should hold its shape. Whisk the egg whites and a pinch of salt to the soft peak stage. Use a metal spoon to fold them into the mixture. Fold in the flour, cornflour and cocoa until evenly mixed. Pour into the cake tin. Bake in a moderate oven (180°C, 350°F, gas 4) for 1 hour, until firm to the touch. Turn the cake out and leave it to cool.

Meanwhile, make the biscuit base. Sift the flour into a bowl. Rub in the butter until the mixture resembles breadcrumbs, stir in the egg yolk, sugar and a pinch of salt. Knead lightly together and chill. Grease the cake tin and reline it. Press the biscuit dough into the base and bake for 30 minutes at the same oven setting. Turn onto a serving plate.

Drain the cherries, reserving the syrup. Set aside 7 cherries. Chop the remainder, and place them in a pan with 6 tablespoons of the syrup. Blend in the arrowroot and bring to the boil, stirring. Remove from the heat and stir in 4 tablespoons of the Kirsch.

Spread the biscuit base with the redcurrant jelly. Cut the sponge in half. Sprinkle both halves with the rest of the Kirsch. Spread the cherry mixture on one half and place the other half on top. Place the cake on biscuit base. Whisk the cream lightly and spread it thinly over the top and sides of cake. Place the remaining cream in a piping bag fitted with a small star tube. Decorate the cake with swirls of cream chocolate caraque, grated chocolate and cherries. The cake can be stored in the fridge for up to 4 days.

SACHERTORTE
8 servings

Sprinkled with rum and filled with apricot jam, this moist rich cake is as good as any slice you could buy in an Austrian coffee house.

150 g/5 oz plain dark chocolate, grated
150 g/5 oz butter
150 g/5 oz icing sugar
5 eggs, separated
150 g/5 oz self-raising flour
25 g/1 oz cornflour
1 tablespoon rum
5 tablespoons sieved apricot jam

Icing:
100 g/4 oz caster sugar
150 g/5 oz plain dark chocolate, grated
50 g/2 oz milk chocolate

Grease and flour a 20-cm/8-in round cake tin. To make the cake mixture, melt the chocolate in a basin with 1 tablespoon warm water. Leave to cool. Cream the butter and sugar together until light and fluffy and gradually beat in the chocolate. Beat in the egg yolks one at a time. Sift the flour and cornflour together and fold them into the chocolate mixture. Whisk the egg whites to soft peaks. Beat 1 tablespoon of egg white into mixture, then fold in the remainder. Spoon the mixture into the cake tin and bake in a cool oven at 150°C, 300°F, gas 2 for 50 minutes to 1 hour until firm to touch. Turn out the cake and cool it on a wire rack. Split the cake in half, sprinkle it with rum and sandwich it together with 2 tablespoons of the apricot jam. Spread the top and sides of the cake with apricot jam and place cake on a wire rack.

To make the icing; Dissolve sugar in 150 ml (¼ pint) water over a low heat. Do not stir. Bring to the boil and boil until the mixture reaches 115°C/240°F (the soft ball stage) on a sugar thermometer (or until a few drops form a soft ball when dropped into cold water). Remove the pan from heat. Melt the plain chocolate and stir in 3 tablespoons warm water. Gradually whisk in the sugar syrup, then beat well until the sauce forms a coating consistency. Pour it over the cake and spread it on with a palette knife. Lift the cake immediately onto a serving plate. Melt the milk chocolate and place it in a greaseproof piping bag. Pipe 'Sacher' across the top.

HOT PUDDINGS AND DESSERTS

CHOCOLATE PANCAKES WITH APRICOT SAUCE

Serves 4

Pancakes freeze very well. Cool cooked pancakes, then stack, interleaved with pieces of greaseproof paper. Wrap them in foil and freeze them. Re-heat from frozen by placing the foil-wrapped stack in a moderately hot oven (200°C, 400°F, gas 6) for 30 minutes.

75 g/3 oz plain flour
25 g/1 oz cocoa powder
1 egg
300 ml/½ pint milk
lard or oil for frying

Apricot Sauce:
210-g/7½-oz can apricots
grated rind of 1 orange

Sift the flour and cocoa into a bowl. Make a well in the centre, add the egg and a little of the milk. Beat with a wooden spoon, gradually incorporating the flour. As the mixture thickens, gradually add more milk. Beat well until smooth. Add any remaining milk and beat well.

Heat a little lard or oil in a 15 to 18-cm/6 to 7-inch frying pan until hot. Pour in enough batter to cover the base of the pan thinly, tilting the pan to make sure the batter covers the base evenly. Cook over a high heat for about 1 minute until browned. Toss or turn the pancake and cook it for a further 30 seconds. Slide it out onto a warm plate and keep warm. Repeat the process to make 8 pancakes in all, adding a little lard or oil before cooking each pancake.

To make the sauce, drain the apricots and pureé them in a blender. Heat the pureé in a saucepan with orange rind. Pour the sauce over the pancakes and sprinkle with toasted almonds. Serve with vanilla ice cream.

CHOCOLATE SOUFFLE
4–6 servings

Don't be frightened of making a hot soufflé—the base is just a chocolate sauce which can be made in advance. Just whisk egg whites and fold them in 45–50 minutes before the spectacular serving to your waiting guests!

65 g/2½ oz caster sugar
50 g/2 oz butter
50 g/2 oz plain flour
75 g/3 oz plain dark chocolate, melted
300 ml/½ pint milk
3 eggs, separated
1 teaspoon sifted icing sugar

Butter a 1.15 litre/2 pint soufflé dish and dust it with 15 g/½ oz caster sugar. Melt the butter in a saucepan and stir in the flour. Cook, stirring for 1 minute until mixture comes away from sides of pan. Remove the pan from the heat and gradually add the milk, beating well between each addition. Bring to the boil, stirring, to form a thick smooth paste. Remove the pan from heat and beat in the sugar and chocolate. Cool slightly then beat in the egg yolks one at a time. Whisk the egg whites until just stiff and carefully fold them into the chocolate mixture, using a metal spoon. Turn the mixture into the prepared soufflé dish and bake in a preheated hot oven (190°C, 375°F, gas 5) for 45–50 minutes until well risen. Do not open the oven door during the cooking or the soufflé will drop. Quickly dust the top with icing sugar and serve immediately with single cream or thick Greek yogurt.

HOT CHOCOLATE CUSTARD POTS
4-6 servings

A creamy, chocolatey custard, very comforting on a chilly evening.

450 ml/¾ pint milk
150 ml/¼ pint single cream
100 g/4 oz plain dark chocolate, grated
3 eggs
1 egg yolk
25 g/1 oz caster sugar
2 teaspoons rum (optional)

To garnish:
Lightly whipped cream, pistachio nuts

Heat the milk and cream in a saucepan with the chocolate on a low heat until melted, but do not let it boil. Beat together eggs, egg yolk, caster sugar and rum, if used. Pour the warmed chocolate milk over the egg mixture, stirring. Strain the mixture into a jug or clean pan and pour it into 4–6 ovenproof ramekins or custard cups. Stand them in a roasting tin then pour warm water into tin to come half way up the sides of the pots. Bake in a moderate oven (160°C, 325°F, gas 3) for about 40 minutes, until lightly set. Serve hot or warm with lightly whipped cream and pistachio nuts.

PRALINE PUD

Moist and nutty—delicious with cream or custard. Why not simmer toasted chopped hazelnuts in the milk before making the custard?

225 g/8 oz butter
250 g/9 oz caster sugar
4 eggs, beaten
175 g/6 oz self raising flour
50 g/2 oz cocoa powder
50 g/2 oz ground hazelnuts

Thickly butter a 1.15-litre/2-pint pudding basin. Beat the butter and sugar together until light and fluffy, and gradually beat in the eggs. Use a metal spoon to fold the flour into the mixture. Divide the mixture in half and fold the hazelnuts into one portion and the cocoa into the other. Place alternate spoonfuls of the mixture into a basin and cover with a double thickness of foil or greaseproof paper. Make a pleat in the top to allow the pudding to rise and tie it with string. Place it in a saucepan of simmering water (which should come halfway up the side of the basin). Cover with a tight-fitting lid and steam for 1¾–2 hours, topping up with water as necessary. Remove the foil or paper and invert the pudding onto a serving plate. Serve with cream or custard.

CHOC MINT SAUCY SPONGE

4 servings

The secret of success lies in cooking this dessert in a water bath. Keeping the bottom layer cool will make the mixture separate into a light sponge topping over a sticky chocolate sauce. If you prefer the bottom layer to have a firmer consistency, bake for an extra 20 minutes.

50 g/2 oz soft margarine
100 g/4 oz caster sugar
25 g/1 oz self-raising flour
2 tablespoons cocoa powder
3 drops peppermint essence
2 eggs, separated
300 ml/½ pint milk
1 chocolate peppermint bar

Lightly grease a deep 900-ml/1½-pint ovenproof dish. Place it in a roasting tin in 2.5-cm/1-inch depth of water. Place the margarine, sugar, flour, cocoa and peppermint essence and egg yolks in a bowl. Beat the chocolate mixture with a wooden spoon until creamy and smooth, then gradually beat in all the milk. Whisk the egg whites until stiff but not dry. Fold them into the chocolate mixture with a metal spoon, until well blended. Pour into the prepared dish and bake in the centre of a moderately hot oven (200°C, 400°F, gas 6) for 25 minutes. Chop the chocolate peppermint bar and sprinkle it over the top. Serve piping hot.

AUTUMN CRUMBLE
4–6 servings

This pudding has a chocolate oaty crumble topping which would also go well with canned peaches or fresh or canned pineapple.

675 g/1½ lb cooking apples, peeled, cored and sliced
1 tablespoon water
100 g/4 oz fresh or frozen blackberries
50 g/2 oz caster sugar

Crumble Topping:
100 g/4 oz plain flour
25 g/1 oz drinking chocolate
75 g/3 oz butter
25 g/1 oz porridge oats
25 g/1 oz caster sugar

Place the apples and water in a saucepan. Bring to the boil, cover, and cook on low heat for 5 minutes. Stir in the blackberries and sugar and transfer to a 900 ml–1.15 litre/1½–2 pint ovenproof dish.

To make the crumble topping, sift the flour and drinking chocolate into a bowl and rub in the butter until the mixture resembles breadcrumbs. Add the porridge oats and sugar and mix well. Spoon the crumble topping over the fruit and bake the pudding in a moderate oven (180°C, 350°F, gas 4) for about 40 minutes. Serve with ice cream.

PINEAPPLE CHOC SOUFFLE OMELETTE
2 servings

A great instant dessert for those meals when you are stuck for inspiration.

1 tablespoon cocoa powder
1 tablespoon hot water
2 size 2 eggs, separated
2 teaspoons cold water
2 teaspoons caster sugar
15 g/½ oz butter
2 tablespoons pineapple jam, warmed
2 teaspoons flaked coconut, toasted

Put an empty 15 to 18-cm/6 to 7-inch omelette pan on a low heat to get hot. Blend the cocoa with the hot water, then add it to the egg yolks, cold water and caster sugar. Whisk together until creamy. Whisk the egg whites until just stiff and fold them into the yolk mixture. Melt the butter in the hot pan, pour in omelette mixture and spread it evenly. Cook over a moderate heat without stirring until the bottom is set and browned. Place the pan under a pre-heated grill for about 30 seconds until the top is set. Place the warmed jam across centre of omelette and fold in half. Slide the omelette onto a warmed plate and sprinkle it with the coconut. Serve immediately.

CHOCOLATE ORANGE FONDUE
Serves 6–8

A friendly way to finish off a meal. The fondue is very rich and filling, so plan the other courses accordingly.

225 g/8 oz plain orange-flavoured chocolate,
broken into pieces
150 ml/¼ pint double cream
2 tablespoons orange liqueur

For dipping:
Marshmallows
Fresh fruit, cut into pieces
Plain cake, cubed

Melt the chocolate with the cream over a gentle heat, stirring well. Remove from the heat and stir in the liqueur. Keep warm in a fondue pot over a gentle heat or in a bowl on a hot tray.

Place the fondue in the centre of table and, using fondue forks, dip in marshmallows, pieces of fresh fruit and cubes of plain cake, etc.

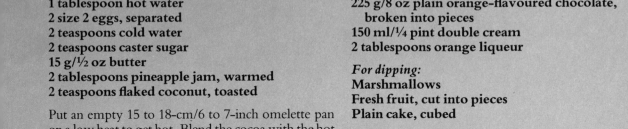

CHOCOLATE BAKED ALASKA

Serves 6

The secret of a successful Baked Alaska is to make sure the ice cream is completely sealed in with meringue.

50 g/2 oz self-raising flour
2 teaspoons cocoa powder
½ teaspoon baking powder
50 g/2 oz soft margarine
50 g/2 oz caster sugar
1 size 2 egg

Filling:
1 tablespoon brandy or Kirsch
4 tablespoons strawberry jam
600 ml/1 pint chocolate ice cream

Meringue:
3 egg whites
75 g/3 oz caster sugar

Grease a 20-cm/8-in sandwich tin with oil and line the base with greased greaseproof paper. Sift the flour, cocoa and baking powder into a bowl. Add the margarine, caster sugar and egg and beat with a wooden spoon for 2–3 minutes until smooth and glossy. (This will only take 1–2 minutes with an electric mixer or 30 seconds to 1 minute in a food processor). Place the mixture in the prepared tin and level the surface with the back of a spoon. Bake in the centre of a preheated oven (180°C, 350°F, gas 4) for 30–35 minutes. Cool on a wire rack.

Place the cake on an ovenproof plate or shallow dish and spread it with the jam. Spoon the ice cream on top and shape it into a mound leaving a 1-cm/½-in border of sponge. Place in the freezer whilst preparing the meringue.

To make the meringue, set the oven at 220°C 425°F, gas 7. Whisk the egg whites until just stiff. Slowly whisk in the sugar until firm and glossy. Completely cover the ice cream and the sponge with swirls of meringue. Bake for 5–10 minutes until the meringue starts to brown. Serve immediately.

COLD DESSERTS AND ICE CREAMS

RICH CHOCOLATE ICE CREAM

6 servings

Milk can be used instead of single cream for a less rich result. Yummy served with easy chocolate sauce (see page 54).

300 ml/½ pint single cream
150 g/5 oz plain dark chocolate, grated
4 egg yolks
75 g/3 oz caster sugar
300 ml/½ pint double cream

Heat the single cream to just below boiling. Remove from the heat, add the chocolate and leave to melt. Whisk together the egg yolks and sugar until thick and creamy, then whisk in the chocolate mixture. Return the mixture to the saucepan and stir over a very gentle heat until thickened, but do not allow to boil. Leave to cool then pour into a plastic or metal container and freeze until the mixture starts to harden at the edges, about 2 hours. Transfer the semi frozen mixture to a chilled bowl and whisk to break down the ice crystals. Whip the double cream until it holds its shape and fold it into chocolate mixture. Pour into a washed and dried container and freeze until required. Transfer the ice cream to the refrigerator 20 minutes before serving.

CHOCOLATE RIPPLE ICE CREAM

6 servings

A rich, creamy ice cream with chocolate running through it. Serve on its own or in chocolate shells (see page 8).

300 ml/½ pint single cream
1 egg
2 egg yolks
75 g/3 oz caster sugar
½ teaspoon vanilla essence
300 ml/½ pint double cream
4 tablespoons cold chocolate sauce (see page 54)

Heat the single cream to just below boiling point. Beat together the egg, egg yolks, caster sugar and vanilla in a bowl. Add the heated cream, stirring. Stand the bowl over a pan of simmering water and stir until the custard thickens. Cool, then pour into a plastic or metal container and freeze until the mixture starts to harden at the edges, about 2 hours. Transfer the semi-frozen mixture to a chilled bowl and whisk to break down the ice crystals. Whip the cream until it just holds its shape, and fold it into the custard mixture. Lightly stir the chocolate sauce through the mixture, leaving ripples. Wash and dry the container and return the mixture to it. Cover and freeze until required. Transfer the ice cream from the freezer to the refrigerator 20 minutes before serving.

MINT CHOC CHIP ICE CREAM

6 servings

An easy-to-make ice cream that doesn't need whisking during freezing. A good, home-made soft scoop.

4 eggs, separated
1 teaspoon peppermint essence
100 g/4 oz caster sugar
300 ml/½ pint double cream
few drops green food colouring
50 g/2 oz chocolate mint sticks, chopped

Beat the egg yolks and peppermint essence together until blended. Whisk the egg whites until stiff but not dry in a large bowl. Add the sugar, 1 tablespoon at a time, whisking continuously until the mixture is stiff and glossy. Whip the cream until it forms soft peaks. Using a metal spoon, carefully fold the yolks, whites, cream, green food colouring and chopped chocolate mint sticks together. Pour the mixture into a container and freeze until firm. Serve with extra chocolate mint sticks.

TIPSY PEAR TRIFLE
4–6 servings

1 large chocolate Swiss roll, cut into slices 2.5-cm/1-inch thick
415-g/14.6-oz can pear halves, drained
150 ml/¼ pint sweet sherry
1½ tablespoons custard powder
1 tablespoon caster sugar
600 ml/1 pint milk
100 g/4 oz plain chocoate, grated
150 ml/¼ pint whipped cream
2 tablespoons toasted flaked almonds
1 glacé cherry

Arrange the slices of Swiss roll in a glass dish. Reserve 2 pear halves for decoration. Chop the remainder and scatter them over the Swiss roll. Pour on the sherry and leave to soak.

Blend the custard powder and sugar with 3 tablespoons of the milk. Heat the rest in a saucepan with the chocolate until melted. Pour the mixture onto the blended custard powder. Stir well and return to the pan. Bring to the boil, stirring, until thickened. Cool slightly, then pour over the pears and Swiss roll. Leave in a cool place to set.

To decorate, slice the reserved pears and arrange on top of the set custard with piped or swirled, whipped cream, toasted flaked almonds and glacé cherry.

CLASSIC CHOCOLATE MOUSSE
4 servings

Quick, simple and delicious. For a change you could try double cream or thick, strained natural yogurt.

100 g/4 oz plain cooking chocolate dots
2 eggs, separated
150 ml/¼ pt carton soured cream

Place chocolate dots in a bowl over a saucepan of hot, but not boiling, water, stirring occasionally, until the chocolate has melted. Remove the bowl from the saucepan. Add the egg yolks to the chocolate, beat until smooth. Whip the soured cream until it just holds its shape. Stir 4 tablespoons of the soured cream into the chocolate until smooth. Whisk the egg whites until stiff but not dry. Using a metal spoon, fold them into the chocolate, cutting through the mixture until evenly mixed. Pour the mixture into a glass serving dish and chill until set. Spoon the remaining soured cream on the mousse and decorate with a chocolate butterfly. (see page 7).

FRUIT CHEESE SHORTBREAD
8 servings

Take your pick of fruit, black cherries, apricots, peaches and mandarins. Lace with the appropriate liqueur, top with cheesecake, and enclose in cocoa shortbread—moist and very more-ish!

250 g/9 oz butter
115 g/4½ oz caster sugar
350 g/12 oz plain flour
25 g/1 oz cocoa powder
2 tablespoons milk
395-g/14-oz can fruit in natural juice
1 tablespoon cornflour
2 tablespoons fruit-flavoured liqueur
225 g/8 oz full fat soft cream cheese
150 ml/¼ pint double cream
1 egg
75 g/3 oz caster sugar
¼ teaspoon vanilla essence
icing sugar

Grease a 23-cm/9-inch round sandwich tin and line base with greased greaseproof paper. Cream the butter and sugar until light and fluffy. Beat in the flour, cocoa and enough milk to form a soft dough. Press two-thirds of the shortbread dough over the base and up the sides of the tin. Make sure the top rim of the pastry is thick enough to support the lid. On a sheet of greaseproof paper roll the remaining dough into a 23-cm/9-inch circle. Chill until required.

Drain the fruit, reserving the juice. Place the cornflour in a small pan. Stir in the fruit juice and cook over a low heat, stirring until thickened. Stir in liqueur and fruit. Allow to cool. Whisk the cheese, cream, egg, sugar and vanilla essence together until thick and smooth. Spread the fruit into shortbread case, top with the cheese mixture and flip the shortbread lid carefully over the top. Remove the greaseproof paper. Press the edges together and bake in a moderate (180°C, 350°F, gas 4) oven for 1¼ hours, or until the shortbread feels firm in the centre. Leave to cool. You may find the crust will crack slightly. Dust with icing sugar and serve cool.

PROFITEROLES
6–8 servings

A much loved dessert, perhaps second in popularity only to Black Forest Gateau. These profiteroles are filled with ice cream, but whipped cream or confectioner's custard can be used instead.

Choux Pastry:
65 g/2½ oz strong plain flour
pinch of salt
50 g/2 oz butter
150 ml/¼ pint cold water
2 size 3 eggs, beaten

Filling:
300 ml/½ pint vanilla ice cream

Chocolate Sauce:
1 recipe easy chocolate sauce (see page 54)

Sift the flour and salt. Heat the butter and water in a saucepan until the butter has melted. Bring to the boil and tip in all the flour and salt. Beat with a wooden spoon over a low heat until the mixture forms a ball and leaves the sides of the pan clean. Cool slightly, and add the eggs a little at a time, beating well between each addition, until mixture is smooth and glossy and just firm enough to hold its shape. Place about 24 teaspoonfuls of the mixture 2.5-cm/1-inch apart on greased baking trays. Bake in a pre-heated hot oven (200°C, 425°F, gas 7) for 15 minutes until well risen, crisp and golden.

Make a slit in the side of each profiterole with a sharp knife to allow steam to escape. Return to the heat of the unlit oven to dry out. Remove from the oven and cool on wire racks. Just before serving, cut each profiterole almost in half, leaving top and bottom hinged together. Fill with ice cream and pile the profiteroles into a pyramid. Pour the warmed chocolate sauce over the pyramid and serve immediately.

MOCHA ROULADE
8 servings

The ultimate dessert. It must be made at least a day in advance. When cooked, it has a sugary crust and sticky centre—worrying the first time you make it but you'll soon realise that's how it's meant to be.

1 tablespoon instant coffee granules
100 g/4 oz plain dark chocolate, grated
4 large eggs, separated
100 g/4 oz caster sugar
300 ml/½ pt double cream
About 50 g/2 oz icing sugar, sifted

Grease a 27 × 33-cm/11 × 13-inch Swiss roll tin. Cut a piece of nonstick baking paper 5-cm/2-inches wider than the dimensions of the tin. Fold over 2.5-cm/1-inch all round. Snip through the corners, press paper in the tin and secure the edges with paper clips.

Blend the coffee to a smooth paste with 1 tablespoon of warm water. Melt the chocolate in a basin over a saucepan of hot water, and cool slightly. Whisk the egg yolks and sugar for 1 minute until thick and pale. Stir in the cooled coffee and melted chocolate. Using a metal spoon, carefully fold in the stiffly-whisked egg whites. Spread the mixture into the prepared tin and bake in the centre of a preheated moderate oven (180°C, 350°F, gas 4) for about 15 minutes. The roulade will have a firm, crisp crust—do not break this—the mixture beneath will seem very moist.

Remove the roulade from oven and cover the tin with a damp tea towel. Leave overnight for the crust to soften.

Whip the cream until it just holds its shape. Place a large sheet of greaseproof paper on a work surface and sprinkle it thickly with icing sugar. Remove the tea towel from tin. Flip the roulade over onto the sugared paper. Trim off the edges of roulade, carefully spread with whipped cream. Roll up the roulade from one short end, using the greaseproof paper to lift and roll. Place on a serving dish and dust with more icing sugar. Serve sliced.

CHOCOLATE BOXES
10 servings

Don't refrigerate the chocolate or it will be too brittle to cut. Let it set in a cool place and cut it while it is still slightly soft—this helps it to break in the right place.

Sponge:
100 g/4 oz self-raising flour
2 tablespoons cocoa powder
75 g/3 oz ground almonds
100 g/4 oz caster sugar
100 g/4 oz butter, softened
1 teaspoon almond essence
2 eggs

Filling and Decoration:
350 g/12 oz plain dark chocolate
150 ml/¼ pint double cream
4 tablespoons raspberry jam
20 crystallised violets or roses and 10 sprigs of green fern

Grease a 20-cm/8-inch square cake tin and line the base with greased greaseproof paper. Place all the sponge ingredients in a bowl. Mix together with a wooden spoon, then beat for 2 to 3 minutes until the mixture is smooth and glossy (1 to 2 minutes if using an electric mixer). Spread in the tin, and level the top. Bake in the centre of a moderately hot oven (190°C, 375°F, gas 5) for 35 to 40 minutes. Turn out and leave to cool.

Line two 33 × 27-cm/13 × 11-inch baking trays with non-stick paper. Melt the chocolate and spread it thinly over the baking trays. Leave it to cool. Cut the cake and chocolate into 5-cm/2-inch squares, to make 16 cake squares and 50 chocolate squares. Whip the cream. Cut the squares of cake in half crosswise. Sandwich 3 pieces of cake together with jam and cream to make 10 blocks. (You will have two squares of cake left over).

Spread one side of the chocolate squares with jam and press them against the sides of the cakes to make "boxes". Place the rest of the cream in a piping bag fitted with a star tube and pipe cream on top of the cakes. Arrange 2 crystallised violets or roses and a sprig of green fern at one corner of each box and place the remaining chocolate squares at an angle on top of the cream to make "lids" for the "boxes".

GOOEY MERINGUE LAYER CAKE
10 servings

Rich and delicious, a must for all chocolate lovers. The meringue rounds can be made up to 1 week in advance. Layer with greaseproof or waxed paper between between each round and store in an airtight container.

Meringue:
4 egg whites
225 g/8 oz caster sugar

Filling:
225 g/8 oz dark plain chocolate, grated
6 tablespoons water
600 ml/1 pint double cream

Decoration:
100 g/4 oz chocolate scrolls (see page 8) or 3 chocolate flakes split into thin sticks

Line 3 baking trays with non-stick baking parchment and mark a 20 to 23-cm/8 to 9-inch diameter circle on each one. Whisk the egg whites in a large bowl until stiff but not dry. Add half the sugar and whisk again until stiff. Fold in the remaining sugar. Spread the meringue within the three marked circles, and bake in a cool oven (110°C, 225°F, gas ¼) until dry and crisp, about 1 hour.

Make the filling two to three hours before serving. Place the chocolate and water in a saucepan and dissolve over a very low heat. Leave to cool. Whip the cream until it stands in soft peaks. Slowly add the chocolate mixture and continue whisking until thick. Place one meringue round on a serving dish and spread with one quarter of the chocolate cream. Place a meringue round on top and spread it with a quarter of the chocolate cream. Place the third meringue on top and coat top and sides with remaining chocolate cream. Decorate with chocolate curls or flake. Refrigerate until required.

CHOCOLATE CHESTNUT CHARLOTTE

8 servings

A creamy dessert that's a winner at dinner parties. This is a good way of using up leftover egg yolks after making meringues.

100 g/4 oz hazelnuts
14 langues de chat, or finger biscuits
3 egg yolks
200 g/7 oz granulated sugar
103-g/4-oz packet plain cooking chocolate dots
200 g/7 oz butter
440-g/15½-oz can unsweetened chestnut purée
150 ml/¼ pint double cream
3 glacé chestnuts
3 chocolate leaves (see page 8)

Toast the hazelnuts under the grill. Rub off the skins in a clean teatowel, and chop the nuts. Line a 1.15 litre/2 pint loaf tin with cling film, leaving sufficient to fold over top. Line the two long sides of the tin with the langues de chat or finger biscuits.

Whisk the egg yolks lightly in a bowl. Dissolve the sugar in 6 tablespoons of water in a small heavy saucepan. Boil the syrup without stirring until it reaches 106°C/220°F on a sugar thermometer, the thread stage. This will take about 4 minutes on high heat. Remove the pan from heat. Place a little syrup on the back of a teaspoon, press another spoon onto syrup, pull apart. If a thread is formed, syrup is ready. Whisk the syrup into the yolks until mixture is foamy; leave to cool. Melt 75g/3 oz of the chocolate in a bowl over a saucepan of hot water; chop the rest. Cream the butter until soft, then whisk it into egg mixture a little at a time, followed by the chestnut purée, the melted and the chopped chocolate and the nuts. Pour into the lined tin, fold the cling film over the mixture and chill until set. When cold remove from tin. Whip cream until thick, place it in a piping bag with a star nozzle and pipe shells over the top of the charlotte. Decorate with glacé chestnuts and chocolate leaves.

MISSISSIPPI MUD PIE
6 servings

To make this cool, crafty dessert, the ice cream must be soft enough to mash with a fork, but not melted.

Biscuit Crust:
200 g/7 oz wheatmeal biscuits, crushed
65 g/2½ oz butter, melted

Filling:
600 ml/1 pint chocolate ice cream, softened
600 ml/1 pint coffee ice cream, softened
2 tablespoons coffee liqueur

Decoration:
Small chocolate flake bar

Mix the crushed biscuits and melted butter. Press into the base and sides of a 23-cm/9-inch flan tin or dish. Chill. Combine the softened chocolate and coffee ice creams and stir in the coffee liqueur. Pour the mixture into the biscuit crust and freeze until solid. Transfer to the refrigerator 15 minutes before serving. Sprinkle with a chopped flake bar, and serve with warmed chocolate fudge sauce.

MERINGUE HEARTS
10 meringues or 20 petits fours

Very crisp and very chocolatey. Pipe them in any shape you like. Small ones will make delicious petits fours.

2 egg whites
100 g/4 oz caster sugar
100 g/4 oz plain dark chocolate, grated

Line two baking trays with nonstick baking parchment. Whisk the egg whites until stiff. Whisk in 1 tablespoon sugar, then fold in the remainder with 50 g/2 oz of the chocolate. Place the mixture in a piping bag fitted with a 1.5-cm/½-inch plain piping tube. Pipe heart shapes, as shown, onto the baking trays. Bake for about 1½ hours or until dry and crisp. Peel the meringues off the paper and cool them on a wire rack. Melt the remaining chocolate and drizzle over the meringues.

CHOCOLATE ALMOND CHEESECAKE

8-10 servings

The cobweb decoration looks complicated but it's really very easy to do. A teaspoon of almond essence can be used instead of almond liqueur. Chocolate syrup, also called Chocolate dessert sauce, can be bought in most grocers.

Biscuit base:
75 g/3 oz butter
225 g/8 oz sweetmeal biscuits

Filling:
2 eggs
75 g/3 oz caster sugar
225 g/8 oz cream or curd cheese
25 g/1 oz ground almonds
150 ml/¼ pint whipping cream
25 g/1 oz cocoa powder
1 tablespoon almond liqueur

Topping:
150 ml/¼ pint whipping cream
4 tablespoons chocolate syrup

Grease a 20-cm/8-inch round loose-bottom cake tin and line the base with greased greaseproof paper. Melt the butter in a small saucepan. Crush the biscuits and stir them into the butter. Press the buttered biscuit crumbs onto the base and sides of the tin. Chill until firm.

Separate the eggs. Beat the egg yolks and sugar until light and creamy. Stir in the cheese, almonds, cream, cocoa and liqueur, then beat until smooth. Whisk the egg whites until just stiff and fold into the cheese mixture. Pour into the biscuit case.

Bake in a moderate oven (160°C, 325°F, gas3) for 30–40 minutes until mixture is just firm. Turn the oven off and leave the cheesecake to cool in the oven.

Whip the cream lightly and spread thinly over the top of the cheesecake. Place chocolate syrup in a small greaseproof paper icing bag (see page 7). Snip off the end of the bag and pipe concentric rings of chocolate on to the cream. To make a cobweb effect, drag a cocktail stick over the surface, in alternate directions, pulling one from the centre outwards and the next from the outer edge inwards towards the centre. Decorate with a chocolate rose (see page 9). Chill the cheesecake for at least 3 hours before serving.

CHOCOLATE TRUFFLE RING
About 20 servings

Rich and chewy, a little goes a long way, making it an excellent buffet dessert. It can be frozen, without the cream for up to 3 months.

450 g/1 lb mixed dried fruit
4 tablespoons rum
150 g/5 oz plain dark chocolate
150 g/5 oz plain cooking chocolate
100 g/4 oz butter
175 g/6 oz Madeira cake, crumbled
50 g/2 oz icing sugar
300 ml/½ pint whipping cream
12 maraschino cherries with stalks

Soak the dried fruit in a basin with the rum for 2 to 3 hours or overnight. Melt the dark chocolate and the cooking chocolate together in a basin over a saucepan of hot, but not boiling, water. Stir until melted.

Stir the Madeira cake into the chocolate with the mixed fruit and icing sugar. Stir until well mixed. Turn the mixture into a greased 900-ml/1½-pint ring mould and press down well. Cover with cling film and chill until firm, preferably overnight.

To serve, dip the mould into hot water for 30 seconds and turn the truffle ring out onto a serving plate. Whip the cream until just thick, and swirl over the ring to cover. Decorate with maraschino cherries. Cut into slices, and serve.

HAZELNUT CHOCOLATE GATEAU

10 servings

An easy-to-make dessert for a dinner party. Make the cake in advance and store it in the freezer in an airtight container for up to three days. On the day it is to be served, soak with sherry, fill and decorate.

Cake
150 g/5 oz self-raising flour
1½ teaspoons baking powder
25 g/1 oz cocoa
175 g/6 oz butter, softened
175 g/6 oz dark soft brown sugar
3 size 3 eggs,
50 g/2 oz hazelnuts, finely chopped

Filling:
2 tablespoons sweet sherry or Cointreau
3 tablespoons apricot jam

Decoration:
100 g/4 oz toasted, chopped hazelnuts
10 chocolate shapes (see page 8)
450 ml/¾ pint double dream

Grease a 28 × 18-cm/11 × 7-inch cake tin and line base with greased greaseproof paper. Sift together the flour, baking powder and cocoa into a mixing bowl. Add the remaining ingredients and beat for 2 minutes, until soft and creamy. Place the mixture in the tin and level the surface. Bake at 170°C, 325°F, gas 3 for 45–50 minutes until well risen and firm to touch. Cool on a wire rack. Cut the cake in half lengthways and sprinkle both halves with 1 tablespoon of the sherry or Cointreau. Sandwich the cakes together with apricot jam. Whip the cream with the remaining sherry or Cointreau until just stiff, spread half of it around sides of cake. Spread the chopped hazelnuts on a piece of greaseproof paper, and press each side of the cake onto the hazelnuts to coat. Spread half the remaining cream over the top of the cake and pipe the remainder around the edge. Decorate with chocolate shapes.

WHITE CHOCOLATE MOUSSE

6–8 servings

Mouthwatering, serve it drizzled with a little whisky, brandy, orange or even coconut liqueur. We like it served with blackberries, raspberries or slices of banana, too.

200 ml/7 fl oz milk
3 teaspoons cornflour
2 tablespoons caster sugar
2 eggs, separated
150 g/5 oz white chocolate
2 teaspoons gelatine
150 ml/¼ pt double cream
6–8 chocolate cups made in paper cake cases
  (see page 9)

Heat the milk in a small pan to just below boiling point. Stir the cornflour, sugar and egg yolks together until smooth. Whisk the milk into the egg yolk mixture, return to pan and heat, whisking custard continuously until it has thickened. Remove from the heat. Finely chop the chocolate and beat the pieces into the custard until smooth.

Place 2 tablespoons of cold water in a small bowl. Sprinkle with the gelatine and stand the bowl in a pan of hot water over gentle heat. Heat until the gelatine is dissolved. Gradually whisk the gelatine into the custard. Whisk the cream until it just holds its shape and fold it into the custard. Whisk the egg whites into stiff peaks. Using a metal spoon, carefully fold the whites into the custard. Spoon the mixture into chocolate cups. Leave to set in the refrigerator.

BISCUITS

PIN WHEELS
About 25 pinwheels

These are easy-to-make biscuits with visual appeal. When taken out of the oven they may still be a bit soft, but they will crispen upon cooling. They will keep in an airtight container for 2–3 weeks.

100 g/4 oz butter or margarine, softened
100 g/4 oz caster sugar
1 egg
225 g/8 oz plain flour
grated rind of 1 lemon
2 tablespoons cocoa powder

Cream the butter or margarine and the sugar until pale and fluffy. Reserve 1 tablespoon egg white, add remainder with the yolk and beat well. Stir in flour and lemon rind to form a firm dough. Divide the mixture in half and work the cocoa into one half. Roll out each piece of dough into a rectangle 25 × 20-cm/ 10 × 8-inches and place the chocolate one on top of the plain one. Starting at one of the long sides, roll up like a Swiss roll. Wrap in cling film and refrigerate until firm, about 30 minutes. Grease 2 baking trays. Cut the biscuit roll into 5-mm/¼-inch slices and lay on baking sheets. Bake in a preheated oven at 180°C, 350°F, gas 4 for 15 minutes until light golden. Transfer to a cooling rack.

CHOCOLATE COCONUT SHORTBREAD
6–8 servings

Crisp and crunchy, this shortbread is irresistible moreish. A definite tea-time treat and without the icing it's good for picnics and packed lunches too.

115 g/4½ oz plain flour
25 g/1 oz cocoa powder
15 g/½ oz desiccated coconut
50 g/2 oz caster sugar
100 g/4 oz butter
1 recipe chocolate glacé icing (see page 52)

Sift the flour and cocoa into a bowl. Stir in the coconut and caster sugar. Rub in the butter with your fingertips until mixture sticks together and forms a firm dough. Press the dough into an 18-cm/7-inch sandwich tin and smooth the surface. Prick all over with a fork. Bake in a moderate oven (160°C, 325°F, gas 3) for 1 hour. Cool in the tin. Spread chocolate glacé icing over the top and leave to set. Cut into 6 or 8 wedges and carefully ease out of the tin.

CHOCOLATE CARAMEL SHORTCAKE

20 fingers

Fingers of melt-in-the-mouth shortcake, topped with chewy caramel and melted chocolate. The combination of plain and milk chocolate gives a pretty effect, but either all plain or all milk chocolate can be used.

Base:
100 g/4 oz butter, softened
1 egg yolk
1 tablespoon water
200 g/7 oz plain flour
1 teaspoon baking powder

Filling:
400-g/14-oz can condensed milk
50 g/2 oz butter
2 tablespoons golden syrup
1 teaspoon vanilla essence

Topping:
75 g/3 oz plain chocolate, grated
75 g/3 oz milk chocolate, grated

Grease an 28 × 18-cm/11 × 7-inch shallow baking tin. To make the base, beat together the butter, egg yolk and water until creamy. Sift the flour with the baking powder and work them into butter mixture to form a stiff dough. Press the dough into the prepared tin and smooth the surface. Bake for 20 minutes in a moderate oven (180°C, 350°F, gas 4). Remove and leave to cool in the tin.

To make the filling, place the condensed milk, butter, golden syrup and vanilla essence in a saucepan. Heat gently stirring occasionally until the butter has melted. Increase the heat and boil for 5 minutes, stirring continuously. Take care not to let the mixture burn. Cool slightly, then spread over the base in the tin and leave to set. For the topping, melt the types of chocolate separately in bowls over a pan of hot water. Place alternate teaspoonfuls of plain and milk chocolate on the set caramel and swirl to spread. Leave to set, cut into fingers and remove from tin.

FLORENTINES
20 biscuits

Make sure you place teaspoonfuls of mixture well apart or they will run together. The spoonfuls must be packed with fruit and nuts too—or the mixture will spread, and have too many holes.

50 g/2 oz butter
50 g/2 oz caster sugar
25 g/1 oz plain flour
50 g/2 oz blanched almonds, chopped
25 g/1 oz glacé cherries, chopped
25 g/1 oz mixed candied peel, chopped
25 g/1 oz desiccated coconut
100 g/4 oz plain dark chocolate, melted

Line 2 baking trays with nonstick baking paper. Melt the butter and sugar in a small pan. Remove from the heat and stir in the flour, almonds, cherries, peel and coconut.

Place teaspoonfuls of the mixture well apart on the baking trays. Flatten them slightly. Bake the biscuits in centre of a moderate oven (180°C, 350°F, gas 4) for 10 minutes, until golden brown. Leave to cool.

Spread the chocolate over the biscuits. Mark wavy lines in the chocolate with a fork and leave to set.

CHOCOLATE MINT BOURBONS
About 20 biscuits

These biscuits freeze well, with or without the icing. Freeze in rigid containers and thaw at room temperature for 2–3 hours.

225 g/8 oz self-raising flour
pinch of salt
25 g/1 oz cocoa powder
100 g/4 oz butter or margarine
100 g/4 oz caster sugar
1 egg, beaten
1 tablespoon water

Butter Icing:
75 g/3 oz butter, softened
150 g/6 oz icing sugar, sifted
few drops peppermint essence
few drops green food colouring

Sift the flour, salt and cocoa into a mixing bowl. Rub in the butter or margarine until mixture resembles breadcrumbs. Stir in the sugar. Add the egg and water and mix to a very stiff dough. Knead until smooth. Roll out the dough on a lightly-floured

surface to a thickness of 3mm/⅛inch. Cut it into 6 × 3-cm/2½ × 1¼-inch rectangles. Transfer these to greased baking trays and prick them with a fork. Gather up the trimmings and re-roll them to make more rectangles. Chill the rectangles on the trays for 30 minutes. Bake them for 15 minutes in a moderately hot oven (190°C, 375°F, gas 5) and cool them on wire racks.

To make the icing, beat the butter until creamy, gradually adding the icing sugar and beating until soft. Add peppermint essence to taste and a little green food colouring to make the mixture pale green. Sandwich the biscuits together with butter icing. Store in a cake tin for up to 1 week.

CHOCOLATE GARLANDS
About 24

These biscuits make excellent presents when packaged in attractive gift boxes. Make sure the packaging is airtight, or the biscuits will go soft. Try piping fingers, swirls and 'S' shapes as well.

225 g/8 oz softened butter or soft margarine
5 tablespoons icing sugar, sifted
½ teaspoon ground allspice
200 g/7 oz plain flour
25 g/1 oz cocoa powder
100 g/4 oz cornflour
1–2 tablespoons milk (optional)

Cream the butter or margarine with 4 tablespoons of the icing sugar until pale, soft and fluffy. Sift the allspice, flour, cocoa and cornflour into the creamed mixture and beat until well blended. Add a little milk if the mixture is too firm to pipe. Spoon the mixture into a large piping bag, fitted with a 1-cm/½-inch star nozzle. Pipe 5-cm/2-inch rings of the mixture onto greased baking trays, allowing room for spreading. Bake in a moderately hot oven (190°C, 375°F, gas 5) for 20 minutes. Leave the biscuits on the baking trays for a minute or so to firm up, then transfer them to wire racks to cool. Dredge with the rest of the icing sugar.

CHOCOLATE HARVEST BARS
18 fingers

A good 'tray-bake' for the family. Unsweetened muesli is used in this recipe but you could substitute the same weight of a mixture of porridge oats, chopped nuts and dried fruit. To measure golden syrup, weigh the tin and remove quantity required.

100 g/4 oz butter or margarine
75 g/3 oz golden syrup
75 g/3 oz soft brown sugar
75 g/3 oz plain chocolate, grated
325 g/12 oz unsweetened muesli

Grease a 28 × 18-cm/11 × 7-inch shallow baking tin. Melt the butter or margarine, the golden syrup, the brown sugar and the chocolate in a saucepan over a low heat, stirring occasionally. Remove from the heat before the mixture boils. Stir in muesli and mix well. Spoon the mixture into the prepared tin and level the surface. Bake in a moderate oven (180°C, 350°F, gas 4) for 30 minutes. Cool in the tin for 5 minutes, then cut into 18 fingers. Leave in the tin until cold.

HAZELNUT REFRIGERATOR CAKE
10 servings

Quick, simple and delicious.

50 g/2 oz whole hazelnuts
100 g/4 oz block margarine
75 g/3 oz caster sugar
2 tablespoons cocoa
1 egg, beaten
50 g/2 oz sultanas
100 g/4 oz wheatmeal biscuits, chopped

Line the base and long sides of a 500 g/1 lb or 750 ml/1½ pint loaf tin with cling film. Heat the grill to medium-hot. Brown the hazelnuts in the grill pan. Rub off the skins in a teatowel.

Place the margarine and sugar in a small saucepan and stir over a low heat until the sugar has completely dissolved. Stir in the cocoa. Remove from heat. Allow to cool slightly, then stir in the egg, hazelnuts, sultanas and chopped biscuits. Pour into the tin and level with a metal spoon. Chill until set. Turn out the cake and mark wavy lines across top with a fork. Serve sliced.

CHOCOLATE DROPS
About 10 drops

These are a little bit fiddly to make but well worth the effort. Sponge drops can be made in advance and frozen, then filled and coated when required.

65 g/2½ oz plain flour
pinch of salt
3 size 3 eggs
75 g/3 oz caster sugar
6 tablespoons apricot jam or orange curd
175 g/6 oz plain chocolate, grated
15 g/½ oz butter

Grease and flour 2 baking trays. Sift the flour and salt together. Whisk the eggs and sugar in a bowl over a saucepan of hot water until very thick and mousse-like and the mixture leaves a trail when whisk is lifted out (if you are using an electric mixer, the hot water is not necessary). Remove from the heat and whisk until cool. Using a metal spoon, carefully fold in the flour until evenly mixed. Spoon the mixture into a large piping bag fitted with a 1-cm/½-inch plain nozzle. Pipe drops about 3.5-cm/1½-inches in diameter, allowing room for spreading. Bake in a moderate oven (180°C, 350°F, gas 4) for 10 minutes, until golden. Cool on a wire rack.

Sandwich pairs of sponge drops together with apricot jam or orange curd.

Melt the chocolate with 2 tablespoons of water in a bowl over a saucepan of hot water. Remove the bowl from the heat and stir in the butter. Balance a sponge drop sandwich on a fork and lower it into the chocolate. Completely cover the sandwich by spooning chocolate over it. Lift it out on the fork and transfer it to a piece of non-stick paper. Repeat with remaining sponge drops. Leave to set, about 1 hour.

DOUBLE CHOC DELIGHTS
30 biscuits

Great chunks of melted chocolate inside crisp cocoa biscuits — double the delights!

175 g/6 oz margarine
275 g/10 oz caster sugar
1 large egg
275 g/10 oz plain flour, sifted
50 g/2 oz cocoa powder
75 g/3 oz bar milk chocolate, chopped
About 3 tablespoons milk

Cream the margarine and sugar together until light and fluffy. Gradually beat in the egg. Fold in the flour, cocoa and chopped chocolate. Add enough milk to give a soft dropping consistency.

Place tablespoons of the mixture well apart on a lightly-greased baking tray. Flatten with the back of a damp spoon. Bake in a moderately hot oven, (190°C, 375°F, gas 5), for 10-12 minutes. Cool on a wire rack. Store in a cake tin for up to 2 weeks.

CHOCOLATE WHEATMEALS
24 biscuits

The favourite dunker with a cup of tea—nice without chocolate too!

275 g/10 oz wholemeal flour
½ teaspoon salt
1 teaspoon baking powder
50 g/2 oz soft brown sugar
175 g/6 oz butter
2 eggs, lightly beaten
100 g/4 oz milk or plain chocolate

Dust 2 baking trays with flour. Place the wholemeal flour, salt, baking powder and sugar in a bowl. Rub in the butter. Add the eggs and mix with a fork, then knead into a stiff dough. Dust a work surface with more flour and roll out the dough to a thickness of 5-mm/¼-inch. Cut out 5-cm/2-inch circles, using a plain pastry cutter. Place on prepared baking sheets. Bake in the centre and just above the centre of a moderate oven (180°C, 350°F, gas 4) for 15–20 minutes, until the biscuits are lightly browned. Cool the biscuits on wire racks. Melt the chocolate in a bowl over boiling water and spread it thinly over the biscuits.

JUMBO CHOC-CHIP COOKIES

20 cookies

Light, crisp and ever so tempting. Use plain or milk chocolate, and add grated orange rind or chopped hazelnuts as a variation.

100 g/4 oz butter
50 g/2 oz muscovado sugar
50 g/2 oz granulated sugar
1 egg, beaten
150 g/5 oz plain flour
½ teaspoon bicarbonate of soda
pinch of salt
175 g/6 oz cooking chocolate dots

Grease 2 baking trays. Cream the butter and sugars together until light and fluffy, and gradually beat in the egg. Sift the dry ingredients together, and beat them into the mixture. Fold in the chocolate dots. Place tablespoonfuls of the mixture about 5-cm/2-inches apart on the baking trays and flatten them slightly. Bake for 10 to 15 minutes until golden. Cool, and store in a cake tin for up to 2 weeks.

BROWNIES

12 brownies

Moist and chewy, an American favourite!

225 g/8 oz margarine
375 g/13 oz caster sugar
1½ teaspoons vanilla essence
4 size 3 eggs
100 g/4 oz plain flour
75 g/3 oz cocoa powder
½ teaspoon baking powder
½ teaspoon salt
100 g/4 oz pecans or walnuts, roughly chopped

Grease, and line the base of a 28 × 18 × 2.5-cm/11 × 7 × 1-inch tin. Melt the margarine and pour it into a large bowl. Add the sugar and vanilla essence. Add the eggs one at a time, beating well after each addition. Sift the flour, cocoa, baking powder and salt and add them to the mixture. Mix well and stir in the nuts. Transfer the mixture to the tin.

Bake in the centre of a moderate oven (180°C, 350°F, gas 4) for 40 minutes. Leave the cake in the tin to cool completely. When cold, cut it into 12 squares.

CONFECTIONERY

NUT CLUSTERS
About 15 clusters

This is a good way of using up leftover melted chocolate after dipping biscuits or sweets.

100 g/4 oz plain or milk chocolate, grated
150 g/6 oz unsalted roasted peanuts, hazelnuts or roughly-chopped brazil nuts

Melt the chocolate in a bowl over a saucepan of hot water. Add the nuts and stir well. Place spoonfuls of the mixture into petit four cases or in heaps on non-stick baking paper or waxed paper, and leave to set.

CHOCOLATE COCONUT ICE
36 pieces

If you don't have a sugar thermometer, test the sugar and milk mixture for soft ball stage by placing a small drop of the mixture into cold water. When rolled with the fingers the mixture should form a soft ball.

450 g/1 lb granulated sugar
150 ml/¼ pint milk
150 g/5 oz desiccated coconut
150 g/5 oz milk or plain chocolate cake covering
25 g/1 oz plain chocolate cake covering

Grease an 18-cm/7-inch square cake tin. Dissolve the sugar in the milk in a heavy saucepan over a low heat, stirring. Bring to the boil and boil gently, without stirring, for about 10 minutes or until the mixture registers 116°C/240°F on a sugar thermometer, the soft ball stage. Remove the pan from the heat and stir in the coconut. Pour the mixture into the prepared tin. Leave for 30 minutes then mark it into squares.

Melt the milk chocolate cake covering in a bowl over a saucepan of hot water. Place a coconut ice square on a fork and dip into chocolate until it is completely coated. Lift it out and hold it above the melted chocolate until the excess has dripped off. Place the square on non-stick baking paper or waxed paper. Repeat with all the coconut ice squares and leave to set. Melt the plain chocolate cake covering in a bowl over a saucepan of hot water. Place in a greaseproof paper icing bag (see page 7) and snip the end off. Pipe a 'Z' on top of each chocolate.

CHOCOLATE CRISPS
25–30 chocolates

Classy, after-dinner chocolates. Flavour the sugar with orange zest or a drop of very strong coffee for variety.

50 g/2 oz granulated sugar
¼ teaspoon peppermint essence
a drop of green food colouring
150 g/5 oz plain chocolate
25 g/1 oz butter
extra sugar for sprinkling

Draw a 20 × 15-cm/8 × 6-inch rectangle on non-stick baking paper. Place the paper on a baking tray. Put the sugar in a small bowl, add the peppermint and green colouring. Stir well. Reserve 3 teaspoons of the mixture. Break the chocolate into pieces, and place it in a dry bowl, over a saucepan of hot but not boiling, water. Add the butter. Stir occasionally until it has melted. Remove the bowl from saucepan. Stir the peppermint-flavoured sugar into the chocolate. Spread mixture evenly over the rectangle and sprinkle with remaining sugar. Chill it until firm but not brittle, about 15 minutes.

Dip a 2.5-cm/1-inch fluted pastry cutter into hot water and cut out chocolate shapes. Alternatively, cut the chocolate into 2.5-cm/1-inch squares.

MR BROWN'S CHOCOLATE FUDGE
Makes 225 g/8 oz

This is a really simple recipe—no need for a sugar thermometer, it's a small quantity so it cooks quickly and easily and is just enough to enjoy without feeling too guilty!

225 g/8 oz granulated sugar
25 g/1 oz butter
150 ml/¼ pint milk
1 tablespoon cocoa powder
few drops vanilla essence

Lightly grease the base of a 600 ml/1 pint loaf tin. Place all the ingredients in a saucepan and stir over a low heat until the sugar dissolves. Bring to the boil and boil for exactly 10 minutes, stirring occasionally.

Remove the pan from the heat. Drop a teaspoonful of the mixture into cold water—it should form a soft ball. If it dissolves instead, return it to the boil for a few more minutes and check again. Remove pan from the heat and allow the mixture to cool for 10 minutes. Beat it vigorously until you hear a slight scraping sound on the base of the pan and the mixture thickens. Pour it into the tin quickly and leave to set.

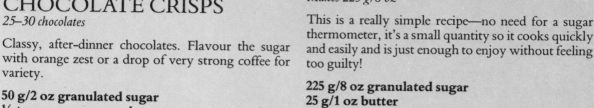

LIQUEUR CHOCOLATES
Makes about 675 g/1½ lb chocolates

Use any combination of three liqueurs you like to make these chocolates. If you follow the instructions carefully you can make chocolates as good as any from the most expensive shop. Use plain dark chocolate couverture (or cooking chocolate which does not require tempering).

450 g/1 lb granulated sugar
2 tablespoons Cointreau
2 tablespoons rum
2 tablespoons Kirsch
275-g/10-oz bar plain or milk chocolate
About 35 foil chocolate cups or moulds

Place the granulated sugar and 8 tablespoons water in a small heavy-based pan and dissolve over a low heat. Bring the syrup to the boil, brushing the inside of the pan downwards with a wet pastry brush to remove crystals around the sides. These could cause crystallisation if they fall in the syrup. Boil until the syrup registers 108°C/225°F on a sugar thermometer, the transparent icing stage. Have ready three small preserving or screw-topped jars. Warm the jars and pour in the hot syrup, *immediately* sealing the lid of each jar, to prevent the syrup crystallising. Open each lid just enough to pour in a liqueur. Then give a gentle shake to let out the air, and reseal. Mix the liqueurs with the syrup by turning sealed jars gently. Cool the jars, first in tepid water, then in cold running water.

Grate the chocolate on to greaseproof paper. Put it into a small bowl and heat it very slowly over a pan of warm (not hot) water to 38°C/100°F (about blood temperature) stirring all the time. Do not allow the bowl to touch the water. Remove it *before* all the lumps have melted, then dry bottom of bowl with a cloth. Allow to cool for 10 minutes, then reheat stirring all the time until it becomes smooth. Try not to beat in any air. Leave for 5 minutes off the heat, give it a good stir, then reheat again. This 'tempers' the chocolate so that it will set shiny and hard.

Fill each foil cup or mould right to the top with the tempered chocolate. Turn the mould upside down over a sheet of greaseproof paper and shake gently or tap, to allow the surplus chocolate to drop out onto the paper, leaving a thin layer of chocolate lining each of the cups or moulds. Scrape off any excess chocolate flat across the top of each cup or mould. Leave the cups or moulds in a cool, dry place for a few minutes to set (not in the fridge, or you'll get condensation). Meanwhile, take the left-over chocolate, including any from the pan, and spread it on greaseproof paper. Leave it to set, then break it in

pieces and place it in a sealed polythene bag. Place the cups or moulds on a level surface ready for filling with the liqueur syrup. To fill them, use a greaseproof piping bag, half-filled with liqueur. Fill each chocolate to within 3-mm/⅛-inch of the top; don't spill any over the sides. Leave for *at least* 6 hours, or overnight. A firm sugar crust should form.

Melt and temper the reserved chocolate as before and place it in a greaseproof paper piping bag. Snip the end of the bag and pipe over each cup or mould, sealing any gaps completely. Leave the chocolates for 10 to 15 minutes to set. When set, invert the cups or moulds and tap or press out gently over a board. If they don't come out easily, chill them in the refrigerator for a further 5 minutes. Place the chocolates in paper cases, handling them as little as possible. Store the chocolates in boxes in a cool, dry place, and eat them within 6 months.

FRESH CREAM LIQUEUR CHOCOLATES
18 chocolates

Professional-looking chocolates that are simple and delicious to make. They will keep for up to five days in the fridge.

100 g/4 oz plain chocolate, grated
6 maraschino cherries
6 pieces glacé pineapple or apricot
6 pieces preserved ginger
150 ml/¼ pint double cream
2 teaspoons icing sugar
2 tablespoons each of four different liqueurs
18 gold or foil-covered petits fours cases (or use a double thickness of plain paper ones to prevent them collapsing)

Melt the chocolate in a bowl over hot water. Using a small pastry brush, thickly paint the insides of the petit four cases with the chocolate. Chill for 10 minutes, then repeat if the coating looks thin in places. Fill each case with a cherry, or a piece of pineapple, apricot or ginger.

Lightly whip the cream until it just holds its shape; stir in the sugar. Divide the cream into four small bowls and flavour each with 2 tablespoons of liqueur. Place the cream into small, greaseproof paper piping bags and snip off the ends. Pipe enough cream into each chocolate case to fill it completely. Place the remaining melted chocolate in a small greaseproof paper piping bag, and snip off the end. Pipe the chocolate over the cream until completely covered. Leave to set. Store in an airtight container in the fridge.

CHOCOLATE PRALINE CONES
Makes about 15

Serve these chocolates with coffee after a special dinner—your guests will be impressed.

15 plain chocolate cones (see page 9)

Praline Filling:
50 g/2 oz sugar
1 tablespoon water
100 g/4 oz blanched toasted almonds
100 g/4 oz plain chocolate, grated
2 tablespoons double cream
1 tablespoon rum (optional)

To make the praline, melt the sugar with the water in a heavy-based saucepan. When dissolved, add the almonds and stir until well coated. As soon as the sugar mixture turns golden, remove the pan from the heat and pour onto a lightly-oiled, heatproof, shallow dish or plate. Leave to cool. Grind the caramelised almonds to a powder in a food processor or with a pestle and mortar.

Melt the chocolate in a bowl over a saucepan of hot water. Stir in cream and rum, if used. When smooth, remove from the heat and stir in the crushed praline. Spoon the mixture into a large piping bag with a star nozzle. Pipe a swirl of mixture into each chocolate-cone. Leave to set.

CHOCOLATE RUM TRUFFLES
Makes 16

A classic chocolate recipe – wickedly tempting. The truffles can also be rolled in cocoa powder or chopped nuts.

100 g/4 oz plain dark chocolate, grated
2 tablespoons dark rum
40 g/1½ oz butter
50 g/2 oz icing sugar
50 g/2 oz ground almonds
50 g/2 oz chocolate-flavoured sugar strands

Melt the chocolate, rum and butter in a basin over a pan of hot water. Beat in the icing sugar and ground almonds. Chill, then roll into sixteen small balls, coat in sugar strands. Chill before serving.

WHITE CHOCOLATE LOGS
36 logs

Irresistable and so easy!

225 g/8 oz white chocolate
150 ml/¼ pint evaporated milk
¼ teaspoon vanilla extract
75 g/3 oz desiccated coconut
2 tablespoons coconut liqueur or rum

Place the chocolate in a small pan with the evaporated milk and vanilla. Melt over a low heat, stirring. Remove from the heat. Stir in 50 g/2 oz of the coconut and the coconut liqueur or rum. Leave to cool. Shape into 30 logs. Coat these in the remaining coconut. Chill until ready to serve.

SAUCES AND ICINGS

CHOCOLATE FUDGE FROSTING
275 g/10 oz icing

Sufficient to coat the top and sides of a 20-cm/ 8-inch cake, or to use as filling and ice the top only. Chocolate Fudge Frosting gives an attractive finish to a cake without the need for piped decoration.

100 g/4 oz plain chocolate, grated
50 g/2 oz butter
1 egg, beaten
175 g/6 oz icing sugar, sifted

Melt the chocolate with the butter in a bowl over a saucepan of hot water. Stir in the eggs and remove the bowl from the heat. Gradually beat in the icing sugar until the mixture is smooth. Allow it to cool until the frosting is thick enough to stand in soft peaks. Spread or swirl it over the cake and leave to set.

CHOCOLATE GLACÉ ICING
225 g/8 oz icing

This quantity is sufficient to cover 10 cup cakes or a 20-cm/8-inch cake. A pinch of cinnamon can be added to give a richer flavour.

225 g/8 oz icing sugar
2 teaspoons cocoa powder
3 tablespoons hot water

Sift the icing sugar into a bowl. Blend the cocoa with the hot water and gradually add this to the icing sugar, stirring until mixture is smooth, and thickly coats the back of a spoon. Use immediately.

CHOCOLATE BUTTER ICING
350 g/12 oz icing

Sufficient to cover the top and sides of an 18-cm/7-inch cake, or to fill the cake and cover the top only. It pipes easily. For plain icing, omit the cocoa and hot water.

100 g/4 oz butter, softened
225 g/8 oz icing sugar, sifted
2 tablespoons cocoa powder

Cream the butter in a bowl using a wooden spoon or electric mixer. Gradually beat in the icing sugar. Blend the cocoa with 2–3 teaspoons hot water and beat it into the icing until you have a smooth spreading consistency. If necessary, add a teaspoon or more hot water.

To make mocha butter icing: use 1½ tablespoons cocoa and ½ tablespoon coffee powder. Blend with the hot water and add to the icing as above.

CHOCOLATE FUDGE ICING
Makes 450 g/1 lb icing

Never stir this icing during cooking or it will go grainy. When cooked, beat it until it thickens. Use immediately as it sets very quickly, like fudge. Delicious!

450 g/1 lb granulated sugar
300 ml/½ pint water
1 tablespoon golden syrup
50 g/2 oz unsalted butter
50 g/2 oz cocoa powder

Place all the ingredients in a large saucepan, blend with a wooden spoon then place over a very low heat until all the sugar dissolves. Bring to the boil, increase the heat, and cook until the mixture reaches 115°C/240°F on a sugar thermometer—the soft ball stage. (To test the mixture without a thermometer, drop a little icing in cold water—it should form a soft ball). Remove the pan from the heat immediately and leave the mixture to cool for about 15 minutes. Beat the icing with a wooden spoon until it is thick enough to hold its shape, very quickly spread over the top and sides of cakes.

EASY CHOCOLATE SAUCE
4 servings

This sauce can be served warm or cold. It will keep for up to three weeks in a covered container. Serve with ice cream, poached pears or profiteroles.

4 tablespoons cocoa powder
4 tablespoons golden syrup
15 g/½ oz butter

Place all the ingredients in a small bowl over a saucepan of hot water until butter has melted. Beat until smooth.

CHOCOLATE MINT SAUCE
6 servings

Grated orange rind can be added instead of peppermint essence. Serve warm or cold with ice cream or sponge puddings.

100 g/4 oz caster sugar
150 ml/¼ pint water
50 g/2 oz cocoa powder
2 or 3 drops peppermint essence

Gently heat the sugar and water in a saucepan, stirring until sugar dissolves. Bring to the boil and simmer for 1 minute. Add the cocoa and beat until smooth. Bring back to the boil, remove from heat and stir in peppermint essence to tase.

HOT FUDGE SAUCE
4–6 servings

Delicious served over vanilla ice cream and sprinkled with chopped walnuts. Equally good served with pancakes, or chocolate steamed pudding.

75 g/3 oz plain chocolate, grated
25 g/1 oz butter
75 g/3 oz soft brown sugar
1 tablespoon cornflour
2 tablespoons water
170-g/6-oz can evaporated milk

Gently heat the chocolate, butter, and sugar together until the chocolate has melted and the sugar dissolved. Mix the cornflour with the water. Add the evaporated milk and cornflour. Bring to the boil, stirring continuously, and simmer for 2–3 minutes until thickened. Serve warm.

CHOCOLATE MARSHMALLOW SAUCE
6 servings

A creamy chocolate sauce, best served hot.

200-g/7.5-oz packet marshmallows
4 tablespoons milk
25 g/1 oz plain chocolate, grated

Chop the marshmallows, using scissors dipped in hot water. Place them in a bowl with the milk over a saucepan of hot water. Stir until the marshmallows have melted and sauce is smooth. Stir in grated chocolate and serve.

DRINKS

ICED CHOCOLATE
1 serving

A refreshing drink for a hot summer's day.

1–2 tablespoons cold chocolate mint sauce (see page 54)
250 ml/8 fl oz cold milk
2 ice cubes

Whisk the chocolate mint sauce and the milk together. Pour the mixture into a glass over the ice cubes. Serve straight away.

AMERICAN CHOCOLATE SHAKES
2 servings

America is renowned for thick, creamy milk shakes. Drink these through wide straws—it will take all day through thin ones.

450 ml/¾ pint milk, chilled
2 tablespoons drinking chocolate
4 heaped tablespoons chocolate or vanilla ice cream

Blend the ingredients together in a liquidiser and pour into chilled tall glasses. Serve with an extra scoop of ice cream floating on the top.

MEXICAN HOT CHOCOLATE
2–3 servings

A warming breakfast drink on frosty winter mornings, or a soothing nightcap before bed.

600 ml/1 pint milk
75 g/3 oz plain chocolate, grated
½ teaspoon ground cinnamon
sugar to taste
2–3 tablespoons double or whipping cream,
  lightly whipped
2–3 cinnamon sticks

Heat the milk and chocolate in a saucepan until the chocolate has melted. Then begin to whisk vigorously until the mixture is frothy. Whisk in cinnamon and sugar to taste. Do not let the mixture boil. Pour into mugs and place a tablespoon of whipped cream on top. Serve immediately, with a cinnamon stick for stirring.

NOVELTIES

SNOWMAN
12 servings

A fun cake for Christmas which the children can decorate themselves.

1 recipe all-in-one chocolate cake mixture (see page 10)
1 recipe plain butter icing (see page 53)
50 g/2 oz desiccated coconut
1 Wagon Wheel biscuit
1 chocolate-covered marshmallow teacake
50 g/2 oz marzipan
Red food colouring, liquorice sticks, liquorice allsorts and raisins for face, scarf and buttons

Grease a 900-ml/1½-pint and a 300-ml/½-pint ovenproof pudding basin. Make up the all-in-one chocolate cake mixture, and place just over two-thirds of the mixture in the larger pudding basin and the remaining mixture in the smaller basin. Smooth the surface of the mixture in each basin, and bake them in a moderate oven (180°C/350°F gas 4). Bake the smaller pudding for about 50 minutes, and the larger one for 1 hour, or until firm to the touch and just beginning to shrink away from the sides of the basins. Turn the puddings out and cool them on a wire rack. Spread half the butter icing over the larger cake and roll it in the coconut. Place it, flat side down, on a cake board or serving dish.

To make the head, cut a small slice from either side of the smaller cake. This will enable the head to sit firmly on the base, and give the snowman a flat top for his hat. Cover the head with butter icing, reserving some icing for sticking on decorations and making snowballs, and roll it in the coconut. Stand the head on the body on one of its trimmed sides, domed side to the front and flat side to the back. Using a little butter icing, stick the Wagon Wheel biscuit on top, and add the marshmallow tea cake, to make the hat. Shape a small piece of marzipan into a nose, and stick it on with butter icing. Colour the remaining marzipan by kneading it with a little red food colouring. Roll it out into a 2.5-cm/1-inch wide strip to make a scarf. Fringe the ends of the scarf and wrap it around neck of snowman. Using butter icing, stick the raisins on for eyes and liquorice allsorts for buttons, and a liquorice stick for the mouth. Roll any remaining butter icing into snowballs. Roll the snowballs in coconut, and pile them up next to the snowman.

FIR CONES
10 fir cones

Freeze these cakes plain, and ice and decorate when required. If you do not have ten moulds, bake the cakes in two batches. If you do not have dariole or castle pudding moulds, bake the mixture in paper cake cases. When cool, peel off the cases, turn cakes upside down, and decorate as below.

½ recipe all-in-one chocolate cake mixture (see page 10)
1 recipe chocolate butter icing (see page 53)
200 g/7 oz chocolate buttons
1 tablespoon icing sugar, sifted

Grease ten dariole or castle pudding moulds. Make up the All-in-one chocolate cake mixture. Half-fill each mould with the mixture and bake in a preheated oven at 180°C/350°F gas 4 for about 20 minutes, or until well risen and firm to touch. Remove them from the moulds and cool them on a wire rack.

Coat the top and sides of each cake with the butter icing. Stick the chocolate buttons in the icing, pointing them upwards to resemble fir cones. Dust the cones lightly with icing sugar.

CHOCOLATE CHRISTMAS TREES

4 Christmas trees

Great fun for the kids to make. Alternatively decorate the trees with chocolate buttons and chocolate flakes.

50 g/2 oz plain dark chocolate, grated
25 g/1 oz Rice Krispies
4 ice-cream cones
25 g/1 oz soft margarine
50 g/2 oz cocoa powder
100 g/4 oz icing sugar
4 2.5-cm/1-inch circles of sponge cake, about
   2.5-cm/1-inch thick
225 g/8 oz marzipan
coloured hundreds and thousands
2 tablespoons icing sugar, sifted

Melt the chocolate in a bowl over a saucepan of hot water. Add the Rice Krispies and stir until coated. Pack the coated Rice Krispies inside the ice cream cones and leave in a cool place to set. Mix the margarine, icing sugar and 25 g/1 oz of the cocoa powder with a few drops of hot water until smooth. Spread the mixture thinly over the ice cream cones and the small circles of cake. Place the cornets upside-down on top of the cakes, so that the cakes form the tree trunks. Knead the remaining cocoa into the marzipan. Roll out the marzipan and cut into 5-cm/2-inch circles, using a fluted pastry cutter. Cut each circle in half, and overlap them around ice-cream cones working from the base of 'trees' to the top, until covered. Spread a little icing on the edges of these "leaves" and decorate with coloured hundreds and thousands. Dust with the icing sugar.

CHRISTMAS GIFT TAGS
Makes 15–20

A novel way to label your Christmas presents. Don't tie them on too soon, though, or they'll go soft. They also make unusual decorations to hang on the Christmas tree.

1 recipe chocolate bourbon mixture
   (see page 40)
cake decorations, sweets, glacé icing, butter
   icing or royal icing for decoration

Roll out the bourbon mixture to a 3-mm/⅛-inch thickness. Using cardboard templates or pastry cutters, cut out shapes such as Christmas trees, stars, bells or holly leaves. Transfer to greased baking trays and make a hole in the top of each shape using a skewer. Chill for 30 minutes. Bake for 15 minutes in a preheated oven at 190°C/375°F gas 5 and cool on a wire rack.

Pipe the name on the tag, then decorate with more piped icing, sweets, or cake decorations (stick these on with a little icing). Leave to set. Tie a piece of thread through the hole, and attach to the gift.

To use as tree decorations: coat biscuits with glacé icing (see page 52) or pipe icing around the edge. Decorate as above and leave to set. Tie thread through the hole, and hang on the tree.

EASTER EGG NOVELTIES

These Easter novelties can be made with home-made or bought chocolate eggs. Fondant icing and egg moulds are available from most cookshops.

To make the Easter Eggs
Polish the inside of egg moulds with cotton wool. Brush the moulds with melted chocolate or chocolate cake covering, invert on to non-stick paper and leave to set at room temperature. Repeat with two more coats of chocolate, to form a thick shell. Use a sharp knife to trim off any excess chocolate around the rim of the moulds. Carefully release the chocolate egg halves from the moulds and stick the two halves together with a little melted chocolate. Handle the eggs as little as possible, to avoid finger prints.

SPRING BOUQUET

Stick shop-bought icing flowers on to the egg with glacé or royal icing and pipe stems and leaves with green-coloured glacé or royal icing. Tie a ribbon bow around the egg.

ROBERT RABBIT

Make the bow-tie and ears from fondant icing. Leave to dry overnight. Cut the teeth and eyes from fondant icing and use chocolate buttons for the centres of the eyes. Make the nose from half a glacé cherry and whiskers from red liquorice. Stick decorations in place with glacé icing.

RED DEVIL

Make horns, eyebrows, fangs and an arm from white fondant icing and stick them on to the egg (they will stick on by themselves). Paint the tips of the fangs, the horns, the eyebrows and the arm with red food colouring. Leave to dry. Cut a tail from red card and stick it on with a little fondant or glacé icing. Cut a fork out of green card and stick in place with the arm. Make the eyes from red jelly cake decorations and silver ball cake decorations, stick in place with glacé icing. Cut a mouth from red liquorice and press it on to the fangs to hold in place.

CANDY CLOWN

Gather a doiley to make a ruffle and stick the egg on to it with a blob of fondant icing. Arrange a ring of Smarties or jelly beans around the egg where it joins the ruffle. Stick them in place with fondant. Make eyes and mouth from white fondant. Make the cross on the eyes with black liquorice and the red lips with red liquorice. Make the nose from half a glacé cherry. Stick the decorations in place with glacé icing. To make the hat, cut a circle of card. Cut a slit from the edge to the centre and shape it into a cone. Secure it with a staple. Fix a sweet on top with a cocktail stick stuck through the point of the cone.

MILLICENT MOUSE

To half a chocolate egg, attach half a glacé cherry for the nose, two chocolate buttons with a little trimmed off for the ears, silver ball cake decorations for the eyes and red liquorice for the tail. Stick in place with melted chocolate and pipe whiskers with melted chocolate.

INDEX

All-in-one chocolate cake 10
American chocolate shakes 56
Apricot sauce, chocolate pancakes with 18
Autumn crumble 21

Baked Alaska 23
Banana and chocolate cake 13
Biscuit crust 33
Biscuits 38–45
Black Forest bars 15
Black Forest gâteau 16
Brownies 45

Cakes 10–17, 58
Candy clown Easter egg 63
Caraque 8
Carob 5
Carob yogurt cake 12
Chestnut:
    Chocolate chestnut charlotte 32
Choc mint saucy sponge 20
Chocolate almond cheesecake 34
Chocolate Baked Alaska 23
Chocolate boxes 30
Chocolate butter icing 53
Chocolate cake, all-in-one 10
Chocolate caramel shortcake 39
Chocolate chestnut charlotte 32
Chocolate Christmas trees 60
Chocolate coconut ice 46
Chocolate coconut shortbread 38
Chocolate cones 9
Chocolate crisps 47
Chocolate cup cakes 11
Chocolate cups 9
Chocolate custard pots, hot 19
Chocolate drops 43
Chocolate-flavoured cake covering 4
Chocolate fruit and nut cake 14
Chocolate fudge frosting 52
Chocolate fudge icing 53
Chocolate garlands 41
Chocolate glacé icing 52
Chocolate harvest bars 42
Chocolate ice cream, rich 24
Chocolate leaves 8
Chocolate marshmallow sauce 55
Chocolate mint bourbons 40
Chocolate mint sauce 54
Chocolate mousse, classic 26
Chocolate orange fondue 22
Chocolate pancakes with apricot sauce 18
Chocolate praline cones 50
Chocolate ripple ice cream 24
Chocolate roses 9
Chocolate rum truffles 50
Chocolate sauce, easy 54

Chocolate scrolls (caraque) 8
Chocolate shapes 8
Chocolate shavings 8
Chocolate shells 8
Chocolate soufflé 19
Chocolate truffle ring 35
Chocolate wheatmeals 44
Choux pastry 28
Christmas gift tags 60
Cocoa 5, 6
Cones made of chocolate 9
Confectionery 46–51
Cooking chocolate 4
Couverture 4
Cups made of chocolate 9

Decorations in chocolate 8–9
Dessert chocolate 4
Desserts, cold, and ice creams 24–37
Devil's food cake 12
Dipping chocolate 5
Double choc delights 44
Drinking chocolate 5
Drinks 56–7

Easter egg novelties 62–3

Fir cones (cakes) 58
Florentines 40
Fondue:
    Chocolate orange fondue 22
Fresh cream liqueur chocolates 48
Fruit cheese shortbread 27
Fudge 47
Fudge sauce, hot 55

Gooey meringue layer cake 30
Grated chocolate 8
Greaseproof paper icing bag 7

Hazelnut chocolate gâteau 36
Hazelnut refrigerator cake 42
Hot chocolate custard pots 19

Ice creams:
    Chocolate ripple ice cream 24
    Mint choc-chip ice cream 25
    Rich chocolate ice cream 24
Iced chocolate 56
Icings:
    Chocolate butter icing 53
    Chocolate fudge frosting 52
    Chocolate fudge icing 53
    Chocolate glacé icing 52
    Mocha butter icing 53

Jumbo choc-chip cookies 45

Leaves made of chocolate 8
Lemon ripple cake 11
Liqueur chocolates 48

Melting chocolate 6
Meringue hearts 33

Mexican hot chocolate 57
Milk chocolate 4
Millicent Mouse Easter egg 63
Mint choc-chip ice cream 25
Mississippi mud pie 33
Mocha butter icing 53
Mocha roulade 29
Mousse:
    Classic chocolate mousse 26
    White chocolate mousse 37
Mr Brown's chocolate fudge 47

Nut clusters 46

Pancakes:
    Chocolate pancakes with apricot
    sauce 18
Pear:
    Tipsy pear trifle 26
Pin wheels 38
Pineapple choc soufflé omelette 22
Piping chocolate 7
Plain dark chocolate 4
Praline pud 20
Profiteroles 28
Puddings and desserts, hot 18–23

Red devil Easter egg 62
Rich chocolate ice cream 24
Robert Rabbit Easter egg 62
Roses made of chocolate 9

Sachertorte 17
Sauces:
    Apricot sauce 18
    Chocolate marshmallow sauce 55
    Chocolate mint sauce 54
    Easy chocolate sauce 54
    Hot fudge sauce 55
Scrolls (caraque) 8
Shapes made of chocolate 8
Shavings made of chocolate 8
Shells made of chocolate 8
Snowman cake 58
Soufflé:
    Chocolate soufflé 19
Soufflé omelette:
    Pineapple choc soufflé omelette 22
Spring bouquet Easter egg 62

Tipsy pear trifle 26
Truffles 50
Types of chocolate 4–5

Unsweetened (Dessert) chocolate 4

White chocolate 4
White chocolate logs 50
White chocolate mousse 37